RELATIONSHIP HELP FOR A BROKEN, BEATEN, AND BATTERED RELATIONSHIP

The 9 Secrets to Transforming a Broken Relationship into a Beautiful Blossoming One

JOHN MARKS

CONTENTS

Introduction   v

1. Nine Steps to Better Communication   1
2. Nine Steps to Better Communication   7
3. Handling A Relationship Conflict   15
4. Rules for Arguing Constructively   21
5. Managing Difficult Situations   23
6. Coping with Relationship Problems   25
7. Managing Problems in your Family   28
8. Managing Problems in your Personal Relationships   31
9. Managing Sexual Problems   34

Afterword   37

Introduction

A solid, sound relationship could be one of the best support mechanisms for your well being and life. Great connections and healthy relationships enhance all facets of your life, from reinforcing your well being to improving your associations with others. If, however, the relationship isn't living up to your expectations, it can drain you completely. Every relationship is nothing less than an investment and requires you to put something into it before it can give you any rewards. The more you put in, the more you can get back. These little things can help you keep a relationship sound, or repair trust in relationships that are seeing rocky times.

Effective Method for Fortifying Your Important Relationships

Every body's relationship is unique, and individuals connect with each other for a distinct reason. However, there are a few things that successful relationships have in common. Knowing the essential standards of sound relationships helps you in keeping them serious, satisfying and energizing in both blissful times and dismal moments alike.

INTRODUCTION

What Contributes To the Making of a Healthy Relationship?

- Staying In Touch With One Another

A few connections appear serene but the people in them do not genuinely identify with one another and cooperate. While the relationship may appear steady on the surface, absence of inclusion and correspondence expands separation. When you have to discuss something imperative, the association and comprehension might never be there.

- Getting Through Clashes

While some couples prefer to discuss and resolve issues, some others may argue and oppose ideas in a stern voice. The key in a solid relationship, however, is not to be afraid of clashing. You have to feel secure so that you can openly express things that trouble you without alarm of your partner striking back, and you must have the capacity to clash without embarrassment, debasement or demands.

- Keeping Other Connections And Diversions Alive

Expecting too much from somebody can put an unhealthy weight on a relationship. Having companions and outside interests reinforces your informal organization and brings new experiences and excitement to your relationship.

- Effective Communication

Legitimate and immediate communication is a key aspect of any relationship. At the point when both individuals feel great communicating their needs, trust and security are reinforced. Nonverbal prompts or body language cues like eye contact, leaning forward, or touching some body's arm are crucial for effective communication.

Nine Steps to Better Communication

Healthy relationships cannot be expected to flourish in a vacuum. They exist between two enthusiastic people who bring their past encounters, history, and desires into them. Each individual is different as far as his or her communication skills are concerned. However, better communication, in light of the fact that it is a skill, can be learned.

The most common misconception about effective communication is that since you converse with your partner, you're consequently conveying important information. It can be stated that communication is either the maker or the breaker of relationships. You can enhance your relationship today by putting into practice some of these tips for upping the level and intensity of communication in your relationship.

1) Stop and Listen

How often have you heard somebody say this or read this in an article about relational abilities? How hard is it to do this when you're "in the minute?" It is certainly harder than it sounds. When we are right in the moment, it is difficult to set aside our point for the minute and simply tune in to what the other person is saying. We're frequently so perplexed about not being listened to that we race to continue talking. In fact, such conduct increases the chance that your partner won't listen, either.

2) Empower Yourself to Listen

You may have quit talking for the minute, but your head may still be caught in its own thoughts. So, you're still not by any means listening to what is being said. Specialists have a system that works extremely well in such a scenario. This system allows them to hear what a customer is trying to tell them. The process involves rethinking what an individual has quite recently said to you. It is called reflection.

Be careful not to do this excessively or in a mocking or ridiculing tone. Utilize the method sparingly, and let your partner know why you're doing it in the event that they ask — "I don't think I'm getting what you're trying to communicate to me and doing this gives me a chance to back my psyche off a bit and truly attempt and hear what you're stating."

3) Be Open and Fair With Your Partner

Some individuals have never been extremely open to others throughout their life. Heck, some individuals may not know themselves or know much about their own true needs and wishes. Anyway, when you are in a relationship, you are inevitably making a stride forward to open up your life and open up your own self to someone else.

Little lies transform into huge untruths. Concealing your feelings behind a shroud of power may work for you, yet it won't work for many others. Imagining everything is okay is *not* okay. Furthermore, giving your partner the silence treatment is about as helpful as giving a fish a bike. These things may have "met expectations" for you previously, yet they are all hindrances to a good communication.

Being open means discussing things you may have never

discussed with another individual before in your life. It means being powerless and genuine with your partner, totally and audaciously. It also means opening your own self up to conceivable damage and frustration.

4) Give Careful Consideration to Non-Verbal Cues

A large portion of our communication with each other in any kinship or relationship isn't what we say, but *how* we say it. Body language is a form of non-verbal communication. It entails everything non-verbal from the tone of your voice, its intonation, eye contact, and how far away you are the point at which you converse with another person. Figuring out how to convey better implies that you have to figure out how to peruse these signs and hear what the other individual is trying to communicate to you. Perusing your partner's nonverbal indicators requires persistence and effort. However, the more you do it, the more adjusted you will be to what they're truly communicating, for example,

- Folded arms in front may mean they're shutting off.
- Lack of eye contact may mean they're not interested in what you're saying, they're embarrassed, or they're thinking something is hard to discuss..
- Louder, more forceful tone may mean the individual is heightening the dialogue and is getting candidly involved in the conversation. It may likewise indicate that they feel not being heard or listened to.
- Someone who's dismissed from you when conversing with you may mean lack of engagement or being shut-off.

At the same time you're perusing your partner's nonverbal

indicators, be mindful of your own. Keep an impartial body stance and tone to your voice, and sit beside the individual when you're conversing with them.

5) Stay Focused

In some cases, talks transform into arguments and then change into a discourse about everything. To be deferential of each other and the relationship, you ought to attempt to keep the conversation centered on the current point of contention. While it is not difficult to get into past shabby deeds or raise everything that a contention appears to call for, simply don't. For instance, in the event that the discussion is about who is making supper today, keep it right to that point. Don't brag or discuss who does what in the house.

Contentions that do veer off have a tendency to heighten and develop into larger issues. One of the two people involved needs to de-escalate the contention, even if that means walking away from it. You must do so as deferentially as could reasonably be expected, saying something like, "Look, I can see this isn't going to show signs of improvement by examining it today. We should think about it and discuss it with a new perspective in the morning. Is that okay?"

6) Attempt to Minimize Feelings When Discussing Crucial decisions

No one can discuss vital, huge matters if they feel defenseless, charged-up, or irate. Those are not the times to discuss the genuine issues (like cash, getting married, having children, or planning for retirement). You may think it is unimaginable, illogical or even conflicting to discuss a passionate subject like getting hitched or having a baby without feeling.

But, these issues need to keep a solid footing of levelheadedness to them to not sparkle over the points that they bring. Marriage, for example, brings together two families, and it involves living with someone else. Having children isn't as charming as buying baby garments and canvassing the nursery. It involves issues like discussing who's going to change diapers, nourish the infant, and be accessible at extremely inconvenient times of the day and night for months.

7) Prepare Yourself To Cede A Contention.

How often do we keep on arguing or have a warmed talk in light of the fact that we basically need to be correct? A large number of couples' contentions spin around one party supposing they're correct and the other party not being ready to cede the point. Actually, both the individuals need to make a reasonable compromise. By doing this, would you say you are surrendering a bit of yourself by trading off and not demanding how right you are? Actually, that is something no one but you can choose.

Would you rather be in a euphoric relationship where you respect the other individual, regardless of the possibility that you might periodically be unable to help but contradict them? Alternatively, would you rather be in a despondent relationship where you know you're generally right? It simply descends to your necessities — if being "correct" is more essential to you than your partner's bliss, maybe you have not discovered the right partner.

8) Fun Loving Nature and Perkiness Help

You don't need to be amusing to utilize amusingness and a fun-loving nature as a part of regular discussions. You simply need to utilize the comical inclination you have and attempt to infuse it into a greater amount of your communication with your partner. Diversion helps in lightening the effect of regular disappointments. Besides this, it also helps in placing things into point of view more delicately than any of the other techniques. This reminds us that even as grown-ups, we all have a side to us that appreciates fun.

9) Don't Just Talk, Communicate!

To impart better and all the more adequately in your relationship, you don't just need to talk. You can convey in different ways — through your movements, and these days, electronically as well (e.g., through email, Facebook, texting, or Twitter). Mostly, couples center just on the talking part of their relationship. However, it is important for you to realize that your movements also talk loudly.

Staying in contact for the duration of the day or week through email or other electronic means reminds your partner that you're thinking about them and how they are a major part of your life. Regardless of the fact that such interchanges are fundamentally fun-loving or insignificant, they can help in lightening your partner's day and enhance their disposition.

A few couples likewise find that utilizing email or an alternate system is less demanding when it comes to examining intense subject matters instead of attempting to do so up close and personal. It's something to consider if each time you attempt and raise a specific subject of discussion with your partner, it transforms into a fight. Email or messaging may be a method for talking about such matters all the more unabashedly and specifically.

Nine Steps to Better Communication

❦

No one is an impeccable communicator. Yet, you can work to improve as a communicator by attempting a couple of the things mentioned in this chapter. All of them may not work for you, nor will they work on all occasions. Better communication, nonetheless, begins with one person endeavoring to enhance, which frequently urges the other to tag along.

KEEP PHYSICAL INTIMACY ALIVE

Human presence is actualized by touch. You can take the example of a newborn child to realize the vitality of a casual, cherishing touch and the effect on your mental and overall health. These profits don't end in adolescence. An existence without physically being in touch with others is a desolate life for sure.

Studies have indicated that a loving touch really helps the body's levels of oxytocin, a hormone that impacts holding and connection. In a relationship between two grown-up partners, physical intimacy is frequently the foundation of a healthy bond. On the other hand, sexual intimacy should not be the *only* reason for physical closeness between two people. Consistent, tender touch—holding hands, embracing, or kissing—is just as critical.

Be sensitive towards your partner's likings and desires. While touch is a fundamental part of a sound relationship, it is critical to comprehend the likes and dislikes of your partner in this regard as well. Unwanted touching or unseemly suggestions can make the other individual worry and retreat, which is precisely what you don't need.

Spend Quality Time Together

You presumably have affectionate memories of when you were first dating your loved one. Everything may have appeared to be new and energizing, and you may have used hours simply talking together or concocting new, energizing things to attempt. In any case, as time passes by, children, work, travel, diversions and different commitments can make it difficult for you to spend quality time together. It happens to all relationships. However, you must set aside a few minutes for yourselves. On the off chance that you don't have quality time, comprehension of each other's feelings and communication begin to dissolve.

Here are some basic approaches to associate as a couple and rekindle love:

- Commit to getting to know one another all the time

Throughout extremely occupied and distressing times, a couple of minutes of truly communicating and associating can help keep bonds solid.

- Find something that you appreciate doing

together, whether it is a pastime, a walk, or a talk over some tea or coffee in the morning.
- Try something new together

Doing new things together can be a fun approach to unite and keep things intriguing. It can be as straightforward as attempting another restaurant or going on a day trek to a spot you've never been to previously.

Couples are regularly more fun and fun-loving in the early phases of a relationship. Be that as it may, this perky state of mind can, in some cases, be overlooked as life difficulties or old feelings of disdain begin to act as a burden. Keeping a comical inclination can really help you get through intense times, diminish stress, and work through issues all the more effectively.

Concentrate On Having a Fabulous Time Together

- Think about fun-loving approaches to astound your partner, such as bringing a bunch of flowers or a most loved film home as a surprise.
- Learn from the "play masters" together. Playing with pets or little kids can truly help you reconnect with your perky side. On the off chance that it is something you do together, you likewise get to know more about your partner, and how he or she jumps at the chance to have fun.
- Make a propensity of laughing together whenever you can. Most circumstances are not as dreary as they appear if you add a bit of humor to your approach.

Figuring Out How to Play Once More

A little cleverness and fun-loving collaboration can go far in calming strained circumstances and helping you see the brighter side. In case you're feeling somewhat corroded, take in more about how fun-loving communication can enhance your relationship.

NEVER QUIT COMMUNICATING

Great communication is a central part of a sound relationship. At the point when individuals quit communicating, they quit relating, and times of progress or anxiety can truly detach you from one another. As long as you are connected by the bond of communication, you can work through whatever issue you're confronting.

Understand Your Partner's Signs

Each of us is different when it comes to level of acceptance and tolerance. Some individuals may react better to sight, sound, or touch. Your partner's reactions may not be quite the same as yours. Understand your partner's prompts, and make sure to convey your own feelings, too. Case in point, one person may appreciate a short back rub after a distressing day while another may very well appreciate a talk over a hot mug of tea.

Such a large amount of our communication takes place in what we don't say. Nonverbal signs, for example, eye contact, inclining advance or moving away, or touching somebody are significant communication signals. For a relationship to work well, every individual must be responsive to sending and getting nonverbal signals. Figuring out how to comprehend this "non-verbal communication" can help you better comprehend what your partner is attempting to say. Ponder on what you are communicating by your own non-verbal signs, and observe if what you say matches what you feel. On the off chance that you say "I'm fine," yet you clench your teeth and turn away, then your body is plainly indicating you are most certainly not fine.

Question Your Presumptions

In the event that you've known one another for some time, you may expect that your partner has a really great idea of what you are thinking and what you require. However, your partner is not a mind reader. While your partner may have some clue, it is much healthier to specifically express your needs. Your partner may sense something, yet it may not be what you require. Also, individuals change, and what you required and needed five years back, for instance, may be altogether different from what the case is now. Getting in the habit of communicating your needs helps you withstand troublesome times, which otherwise may lead to expansion of hatred, misconstruing, and outrage.

Use Your Senses

The most ideal approach to lessen stressful issues rapidly and dependably is through your senses. At the same time, each individual reacts diversely to stress, so you have to discover things that are mitigating to you.

HEALTHY ASSOCIATIONS ARE BASED ON Give-and-Take

If you are hoping to get a 100% return on what you have given in, then you can expect to get disappointed and frustrated in the long run. A healthy relationship is nothing less than a balanced trade off, and each individual needs to play a part to verify that there is a sensible trade.

Perceive What's Imperative to Your Partner

Comprehending what is really essential to your partner can go far towards building goodwill and an environment of trade off. On the other side, it is likewise essential for your partner to perceive your needs and for you to state them clearly.

Don't Make "Winning" Your Objective

On the off chance that you approach your partner with the demeanor that things must be as per your direction, it will be hard to achieve a trade-off. Once in a while this disposition hails from not having your needs met while you were a child, or it could be from years of collected disdain developing in your current relationship. It's okay to have solid feelings about something. However, your partner should be heard, too. You are more likely to get your needs met if you regard what your partner needs, and trade off when you can.

Figure Out How to Deferentially Manage Clash

Clash is certain in any relationship, yet to keep a relationship solid, both individuals need to feel they've been listened to. The objective is not to *win*, but to solve the clash with deference and affection.

- Communicate that you are reasonable and open for discussion.
- Don't assault somebody specifically; utilize "I" statements to convey how you feel.

- Don't drag old contentions into the mix.
- Keep your focus on the issue close by, and regard the other individual's feelings just as much.

Expect Good and Bad Times

It's paramount to realize that there are good and bad times in every relationship. You won't always be on the same page. Frequently one partner may be battling with an issue that hassles them, for example the passing away of a relative or friend. Different occasions, in the same way as employment misfortune or extreme well being issues, can influence both partners and make it hard to identify with one another. You may have distinctive thoughts about managing funds or raising kids. Distinctive individuals adapt to problematic scenarios in an unexpected way, and error can quickly turn to disappointment and annoyance.

- Don't take out your frustration on your partner. Life hassles can make us touchy. In the event that you are adapting to a considerable measure of anxiety, it may appear simpler to snap at your partner. Battling like this may at first feel like a discharge, yet it gradually harms your relationship. Discover different approaches to vent your resentment and disappointment.
- Some issues are greater than both of you. Attempting to constrain an answer can result in considerably more problems. Each individual works through issues in his or her own specific way.

Keep in mind that you are partners, in good and in bad.
- Be open to change. Change is inevitable in life, and it will happen whether you run with it or battle it. Adaptability is crucial to adjust to change that is continually occurring in any relationship, and it permits you to develop together through both the great times and the terrible.
- Don't overlook issues. Whatever issues emerge in a relationship, it is paramount to face them together as a couple. In the event that a part of the relationship quits meeting expectations, don't essentially disregard it. Instead, address it with your partner. Things change, so react to them together as they do.

MANY COUPLES CONCENTRATE ON THEIR RELATIONSHIP JUST when there are particular, unavoidable issues to deal with. Once the issues have been determined, they regularly switch their concentration again to their professions, children, or daily errands. But relationships require constant nurturing and affection to thrive. As long as the soundness of a relationship is essential to you, it is going to require your consideration and care.

Handling A Relationship Conflict

Healthy or unhealthy, there is no such thing as a relationship without conflict. Clash is a fundamental part of being connected with people and with society in general. It exists as an actuality in any relationship, and it is not as terrible as it is believed to be. Truth be told, an association with no evident clash may be unhealthier than the one with regular clash. Clashes are basic occasions that can either debilitate or fortify a relationship. They might be profitable in making deeper comprehension, closeness and appreciation, or they could be damaging, bringing on hatred, threat and separation.

STYLES OF CONFLICT RESOLUTION

Different people react differently. Therefore, when a couple is faced with a clash, people may react in one of the following ways:

- Keeping away from or preventing the presence of clash.

- Giving in instead of battling through the clash.
- Frantically accusing the other individual the other individual.
- Utilizing one's energy and impact to control and "win" the clash.
- Pretending to compromise, yet secretly manipulating to win more ground.
- Looking for a reasonable, ideal answer for both parties. This is an imaginative integrative method, and by far the healthiest.

THREE TYPES OF HEALTHY SOLUTIONS

- Win-win

Most clashes are in regard to subjects that have more than two options. In the event that you dislike the decision your partner's needs, and your partner does not like your decision, with somewhat more exertion you may have the capacity to discover an alternate option that you both like and need.

- No Lose

If you can't find a middle path, then you must search for an alternative that is satisfactory to both of you, or arrange a pleasant bargain. Neither one nor the other gets all that he/she needed. However, each one gets enough to be fulfilled.

- Win-lose

At the point when the clash is over an issue that has just two decision options, one person will get what he/she needs and the other won't. There will be a champ and a loser. In the event that you are reasonable with one another and a large a fraction of time each one gets your own particular needs met, it will be less demanding for each of you when one "loses." Also, it should be an unsaid rule that if one gets what he or she wants on one event, then the other will get his choice to make on another.

Solid Conflict Resolution requires clever management. Yet, it is not easy to apply and utilize reliably. However, it does get to be simpler once the aptitudes and trust are created. Both partners must view their clashes as an issue to be tackled by them. It isn't getting the best arrangement for *me*, but it is about discovering the best answer for *us*. They must earnestly take part and take the responsibility to buckle down together to discover results that are reasonable and worthy to both.

On the off chance that you minimize or negate your life partner's position, or in the event that you dependably get your direction, you will harm your relationship. Your absence of affectability, thought, and appreciation of your mate's position will result in harmed and seething disdain. In the event that fear and force are utilized to win, the relationship will be mortally injured.

On the off chance that you are simply a willing supplier, always attempting to keep your life partner euphoric by fulfilling his/her needs and dodging a clash, you will likewise harm your relationship. You will incidentally educate your companion to be uncaring to your needs and self-serving at your cost. Your respect towards oneself and your self-esteem will disintegrate. Disdain will rot, harming you and the relationship.

REQUIREMENTS FOR HEALTHY CONFLICT RESOLUTION

Begin with the right attitude. Approach the clash as two equivalents cooperating to tackle an issue. Don't be so gotten up to speed with your quick need that you dismiss and overlook your more vital need of having a long, sound relationship. On the off chance that you are too angry to control your emotions and stay in the moment, let yourself cool off before getting into a conversation about the issue.

Taking care of a clash with a friend or family member, or somebody you need to have a great, long association with is different from arguing with somebody who couldn't care less about your needs. With a friend or family member, you must be concerned about his/her best efforts. You both ought to be open, fair and aware, not beguiling, manipulative or ill-bred. Shared trust is a vital issue in a sound, long-haul relationship and neither of the partners should do anything to debilitate it.

There are some attitudes that will practically guarantee failure. These include being negative or suspicious, feeling that you must win at all costs or risk losing face, being stubborn, or being too delicate and afraid to put your feelings out there.

Stages of Healthy Conflict Resolution

Recognize the issue or issues. Have a talk to comprehend both sides of the issue, clashes, needs, and favored conclusions. Clarify to one another precisely what the clash or issue includes. This is the starting stage where you say what you need, and you listen to what your partner needs. The objective at this stage is for you each to express what you each need and to comprehend what the other needs. Use "I" message dialect and avoid the faulting messages. Additionally, utilize your dynamic listening abilities when your partner shares their side.

Create a few conceivable results. This is the imaginative and integrative part. Both of you will agree to certain facts and objectives. From there, search for a few choices that may tackle the issue. Brainstorm all the ideas you can think of, no matter how wild or unlikely. Abstain from assessing and judging every thought until it looks as if no more are going to be proposed.

Assess the option results. Consider each recommended result and take out those that are not acceptable to either of you. Narrow them down to one or two that appear to be best for you both. At this stage, you both must be fair and have the capacity to say things like, "I wouldn't be content with that," or "I don't imagine that would be reasonable for me."

Choose the best result. Select the option that is commonly satisfactory to both of you. Make sure you share the duty of choosing the outcome.

Actualize the result. It is one thing to land at a choice and an another to complete it. At times, it is important to discuss how it is to be executed. Who is to do what and by when?

Evaluate and assess progress. Not all concurred upon results end up being at par with what was first anticipated. Make it a standard to ask your partner how the result is functioning and how he/she feels about it. Something may have been disregarded, misconceived, or something surprising may have happened. Both of you ought to have the knowledge that choices are constantly open for update, yet that changes must be agreed upon.

COMMON MISTAKES

Conflict management can be rather tricky and you can make some common mistakes like:

- Not examining with your partner the system used to resolve your clashes.

- Centering excessively on what you could lose and insufficiently on what you both could win.
- Accepting the other individual must lose for you to win.
- Accumulating extra issues before solving the one you began with.

In the event that you stay genuine to your partner and genuine to yourself, you ought to have a great, sound relationship.

Rules for Arguing Constructively

Arguments can be constructive. Yes, you read that right! The good or the bad that arguments may bring into the equation with your partner mainly depends on your approach and mindset. Here are a few tips for you to turn arguments into tonics for your relationship. They may be bitter at times, but they can reap sweet benefits to you and your relationship in general.

Dos:

- Devote sooner rather than later to determining the issue
- Know why you are arguing before you begin
- Speak generally about what you feel
- Stick to the matter at hand
- Sit down and reach out to the problem
- Agree to disagree in the event that you can't concur
- Acknowledge when the other individual makes a legitimate point

- Stop contending and separate if there is any possibility of physical or emotional violence

Don'ts

- Behave forcefully or insolently
- Argue deliberately to offend the other person
- Generalize
- Bring up old questions or situations
- Walk away without choosing when your dialogue will be continued
- Bring other individuals' presumptions in
- Argue about something for longer than 60 minutes
- Argue late in the evening or in the wake of drinking

Managing Difficult Situations

❦

Relationship issues appear to be excessively unpredictable or overpowering for a couple to handle on their own. All things considered, it is imperative to ask for help when situations get out of control. There are various alternatives that are available to you, including:

- Counseling

A relationship is a huge investment on a personal level. It requires a good amount of focus, energy and commitment on the part of both the individuals involved. However, you should think about couples or marriage counseling to resolve your disparities, if nothing else seems to work. Both parties need to be eager and ready to genuinely communicate what they need, confront the issues that emerge, and afterward roll out the fundamental improvements. For best results, it is important to ensure that both the individuals are comfortable with the counselor.

- Spiritual Guidance

A few couples profit from spiritual guidance of a religious figure. This has a tendency to work best if both individuals have the same basic spiritual beliefs, comparable feelings of confidence and have a good association with the counselor.

- Building Emotional Intelligence

You can consider reading articles, features, and sound contemplations intended to help you put the abilities of brainpower and communication into practice.

- Individual Help

Some people may require special attention, especially if they are battling a serious issue or problem. Case in point, somebody who is lamenting the passing away of a friend or family member may need advice to help him or her come out of the misery. On the off chance that your cherished one needs help, don't feel like you are a disappointment for not giving him or her all that he or she needs. Nobody can satisfy everybody's needs, and getting help may save your relationship.

Coping with Relationship Problems

Relationships, whether family or love – might be an incredible wellspring of affection, joy, backing, and fervor. Notwithstanding, social and personal bonds can additionally be a wellspring of misery and anguish. This chapter aims to help you deal with relationship issues and advice you on how you can make them better.

ACKNOWLEDGE THE DIFFERENCE

Individuals in effective relationships don't attempt to drive others to be precisely like them; they work to acknowledge distinction, especially when this contrast is significant.

KNOW YOUR BOUNDARIES

Individuals are mindful that there is a point where they stop and the other individual starts. Others cannot tackle all our issues or help in spite of the fact that, now and again, we may trust them for this.

. . .

Value Your Present

When relationships concentrate on past occasions, or are built on the hope that things will be better tomorrow, they have a tendency to go off the rails.

Regard Individual Choice

It is acknowledged that every individual has the right to choose his or her heading in life. Any relationship then adjusts to take after this.

Ability to Negotiate

Once each individual has chosen what they need, the couple or family can work out an approach to satisfy these diverse objectives without anybody needing to surrender totally.

Extend Positive Feelings

In a few relationships, this may be sexual closeness. It can also simply be agreeableness.

It may appear that a relationship requires a considerable amount of individual aptitude and independence, which could be a bit off-putting from the start. Relationship issues frequently emerge slowly. By the time we acknowledge them, we may find that we have lost our own particular self-confidence and the feeling of our individual worth. It may be on the grounds that we are in trouble, and this is putting a lot of weight on our relationships or it may be because we have had grievous encounters in past relationships and we have briefly lost our capacity to trust.

We may have been distant with our capacity to make fruitful relationships for so long that we may question whether we ever had the capability. Notwithstanding, most individuals appear to have the capacity to recuperate these aptitudes if they put their brain to it. Much chipping away at enhancing a relationship can begin with the single person. In the event that a person is clear about what they need, as a couple, and steadier about how they request it, the entire relationship can start to proceed onward to a better result.

Managing Problems in your Family

Family issues might be hard to see as there may be quite a few people included. Likewise, a vast majority of us are not used to looking at our families, in an objective manner. We have a tendency to think that they are simply our family, and that is the manner in which it is. Then again, a bit of reflection and investigation can take the heat out of a great deal of troublesome circumstances.

TRY AND CONSIDER WHAT YOU ARE ATTEMPTING TO Accomplish

Assume the best about your own self and ascribe the best thought processes to your conduct. Get together all cases you can think of where the arrangement has worked for others and so on. Possibly get a companion to help you. You don't need to record it, simply think it through. In the event that, as of right now, you understand that you are doing the wrong thing, you may need to make a withdrawal! Notwithstanding, we will expect that you end up persuaded that you realize what you are doing, and you have a bit of proof to back this up.

Think Why Your Family Is Contradicting You

There may be more than one reason for this. Perhaps they don't comprehend your arrangement, or possibly they had a strategy chosen for you. Perhaps, they have a few stresses and nerves of their own. Endeavor to imagine that you are in their place, even though their conduct may be extremely disappointing to you. Envision talking about the problem with them. Consider what they may say and how they may answer. When you know what may be stressing them, think inventively of methods for consoling them. In the event that it helps, make an arrangement for their stresses and consolations.

Examine the Issues

That is simple if your family are talkers, yet numerous families aren't. In any case, you can even now find a chance to serenely specify your arrangements, to give a couple of instances that involve others who have done the same, to reassure their apprehensions, and to sympathize with their bafflement. You may need to drop your focuses into the discussion over a period. Don't expect an overnight occurrence. Individuals rarely change their assumptions that quickly. Don't feel you need to have all their attention to make an impact. Stop the dialogue while the going is great and return to it a couple of days after. This will prove to them that you are not kidding and that some of their stresses have been considered; they will probably be a bit more agreeable the next time.

Managing Problems in your Personal Relationships

Extensive courses have been made to investigate the boundless many-sided quality of human relationships. Issues can emerge from an incredible number of sources, and it can habitually call for some forethought to help unravel the mixture of impacts. These issues could be heightened by the weights from others to structure or end a relationship. The general weights from the media, which give a glorified perspective of couples, regularly conflicts with the actuality that most individuals experience. Here are some basic rules to help you investigate and resolve pressures which you may be feeling about your personal relationships.

Do You Know What You Are Searching For?

There are numerous purposes behind entering into a relationship. Examples include camaraderie, sexual experience, having a long-haul partner, and making a family. Do you know what you are searching for? Have you examined this with your partner? If not, there is a possibility that you might be searching for different things and run into a problem with miscommunication.

Are You Asking a Lot or Expecting Excessively Little from Your Relationship?

A great relationship can give help, sexual representation, fellowship and, in the long run, a chance to fabricate a joint life. In the event that you are looking to it to give more than this (in this case, to provide for you a feeling of reason and worth, or secure you from some profound alarm), you may be attempting to get a partner to give things that actually no one but you can attain.

In the event that, then again, a relationship brings you persistent despondency and misery, you may be tolerating for yourself far less than you have a right to anticipate. For instance, nobody should be suffering because of emotional, physical, or sexual roughness. Do a search for the help you need to change or even end a relationship if any kind of abuse is happening to you.

Have You Gotten a Model for the Relationship You Are Attempting To Construct?

Numerous individuals think that they are accommodating to picture a relationship that they respect and for which they yearn. It may be the relationship of somebody you know or an anecdotal one. Consider how the individuals in their relationship resolve contrast and challenges. On the off chance that it is not clear and the relationship is a genuine one, ask them. Moreover, if they have never been seen to have any issues, possibly that relationship is not a frightfully reasonable model when it is all said and done! Discovering such a model might be an especially troublesome and paramount assignment for gay and lesbian couples.

Can You Discuss Issues?

In all associations, there are going to be times of genuine contradiction, where a clash of wills must be determined. This does not imply that there is an issue with the relationship. Be that as it may, contending the point and arriving at understanding does take a bit of aptitude and practice.

Numerous relationship instructors propose that the most ideal approach to resolving a relationship issue is to speak up for 15 minutes about your perspective of the issue. The other individual listens without interfering except to clarify points. At that point, you swap over, and the other individual takes a comparable time to clarify his or her perspective. At last, take 30 minutes to talk together to check whether you can resolve the issue. On the off chance that you don't succeed this time, come back to the problem a couple of days after and attempt once more.

In the event that you are not in the habit of talking about your relationship, it may be fascinating to try it out. Connections are one of the inquisitive gimmicks of human presence and could be well worth investigating.

Managing Sexual Problems

Nobody would anticipate that a tyke will talk fluidly without needing to learn and practice. Most individuals would be shocked if the Halls of Residence just provided for one option for breakfast, or if all people were required to dress the same. Customarily, individuals hope to have great days and terrible days in the matter of working or performing a game. Notwithstanding, in terms of sex, we tend to overlook that we are all human and all diverse, and we hope to have as instant aptitude, absolute similarity, and complete consistency.

A relationship advisor once noted down what helped his customers resolve their sexual contrasts. He discovered that the biggest number of customers profited by being given consent – to discuss sex, to express their emotions, and to be as they were. Restricted data helped the second gathering of customers – data about the extent of human sexual reactions and about how certain issues went back and forth. Particular recommendations about diverse methodologies, positions or procedures, were the third most accommodating remedial device. For the last gathering of customers whose issues were not helped by these procedures, he offered concentrated help. He alluded to the methodology as PLISSIT for short, and it has turned into the premise for much sexual treatment. Use it to tackle your own particular sexual challenges:

Consent

Provide for yourself permission to consider sex, to fantasize about it, to discuss it, and to acknowledge that it is splendidly okay for you to have your own particular likes and abhorrences. Unfortunately, numerous individuals possess the belief that it isn't right to have sexual sentiments and longings. Most individuals find that their sexuality is upgraded when they quit making rules about what they and their partners *should* like and start to consider what they really *do* appreciate. We need to keep our sexual exercises inside the limits of what is protected and what does not debilitate the opportunity of others. Nonetheless, that does not imply that we need to straitjacket our reasoning.

Restricted Information

Lack of awareness sustains numerous sexual challenges. Most individuals can hope to encounter a misfortune of sexual yearning when they are pushed. The concurrent climax perpetually delineated by movie producers and authors is not the knowledge of the larger part of couples. Most individuals' sexual craving and inclinations change as they develop and become more established. Absence of information about contraception and sexually transmitted maladies can prompt incredible sadness when an unwanted, but preventable, event happens.

. . .

Particular Suggestions

Numerous troubling sexual issues, for example, torment on intercourse, failure to accomplish climax, or erectile issues, can be helped by basic changes in sexual routine or position. Books, a visit to the doctor, discussions with companions and so forth might all help you discover these proposals. You might likewise wish to speak to a sex specialist.

Therapy

The term sex treatment raises most individuals' nervousness levels really high! Notwithstanding, this nervousness is lost as sex treatment is not the obtrusive or uncovering manifestation of medicine that most tabloids claim it to be. Don't let these alarming myths stop you from discovering the help you require. Issues are ordinarily determined by method for exchange, the giving of suitable data about human sexual working and by straightforward behavioral undertakings which are implemented by customers in the privacy and protection of their own home between sessions.

Despite the fact that restraint and lack of awareness are a significant reason for sexual issues, some individuals end up trapped in an alternate manner. They have gotten used to bizarre sexual conduct, which can start to leave them feeling disappointed and perhaps socially disengaged.

Afterword

Relationships are the best part of life. They allow you to learn so much about yourself and grow as an individual; in addition, they allow you to be a contribution to another person's life so that they can become a better person, and a contribution to your life. By growing together, it allows both of you to have more fun, enjoy each others' company, and most importantly understand one another at a much deeper level. Each day put in some time toward your relationship because as with anything else, they take time and effort to continue to blossom.

www.ingramcontent.com/pod-product-compliance
Lightning Source LLC
Chambersburg PA
CBHW070037040426
42333CB00040B/1701